WILD
BRUNCH

Poems About How Creatures Eat

David L. Harrison • Illustrated by Giles Laroche

Charlesbridge

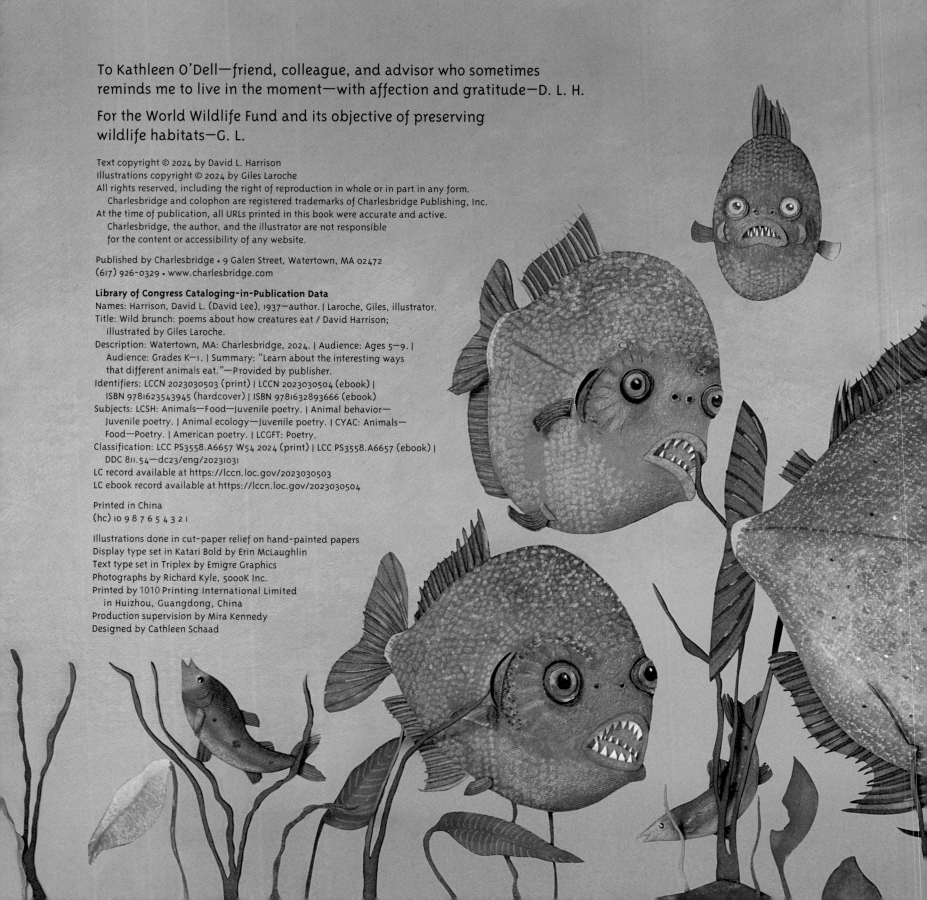

To Kathleen O'Dell—friend, colleague, and advisor who sometimes reminds me to live in the moment—with affection and gratitude—D. L. H.

For the World Wildlife Fund and its objective of preserving wildlife habitats—G. L.

Published by Charlesbridge • 9 Galen Street, Watertown, MA 02472
(617) 926-0329 • www.charlesbridge.com

Library of Congress Cataloging-in-Publication Data
Names: Harrison, David L. (David Lee), 1937—author. | Laroche, Giles, illustrator.
Title: Wild brunch: poems about how creatures eat / David Harrison;
   illustrated by Giles Laroche.
Description: Watertown, MA: Charlesbridge, 2024. | Audience: Ages 5—9. |
   Audience: Grades K—1. | Summary: "Learn about the interesting ways
   that different animals eat."—Provided by publisher.
Identifiers: LCCN 2023030503 (print) | LCCN 2023030504 (ebook) |
   ISBN 9781623543945 (hardcover) | ISBN 9781632893666 (ebook)
Subjects: LCSH: Animals—Food—Juvenile poetry. | Animal behavior—
   Juvenile poetry. | Animal ecology—Juvenile poetry. | CYAC: Animals—
   Food—Poetry. | American poetry. | LCGFT: Poetry.
Classification: LCC PS3558.A6657 W54 2024 (print) | LCC PS3558.A6657 (ebook) |
   DDC 811.54—dc23/eng/20231031
LC record available at https://lccn.loc.gov/2023030503
LC ebook record available at https://lccn.loc.gov/2023030504

Printed in China
(hc) 10 9 8 7 6 5 4 3 2 1

Illustrations done in cut-paper relief on hand-painted papers
Display type set in Katari Bold by Erin McLaughlin
Text type set in Triplex by Emigre Graphics
Photographs by Richard Kyle, 5000K Inc.
Printed by 1010 Printing International Limited
   in Huizhou, Guangdong, China
Production supervision by Mira Kennedy
Designed by Cathleen Schaad

How Creatures Eat

The world is full of animals, and they need to eat. They don't all enjoy the same food, though. What may be yummy to a piranha in a South American stream would not impress a leaf-loving koala up a eucalyptus tree in Australia. And a vulture dining on rotten roadkill by a highway in Kansas has a menu all its own. Animals have developed different ways to satisfy their appetites. A jellyfish snags its next meal without even seeing it. An elephant uses its tusks to dig and its trunk to grab bark and leaves and shovel them down its enormous mouth. Many a fly has failed to outwit a hungry bat tracking it through the evening air. This book introduces some of the world's most interesting ways that animals eat what they eat.

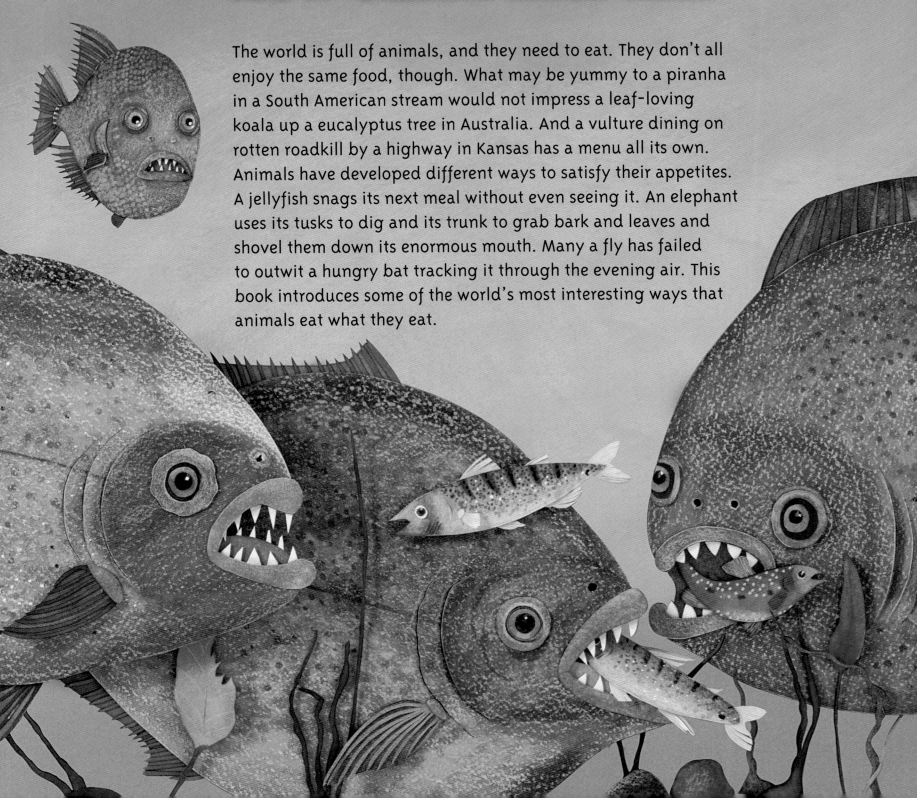

SWIMMING EATERS

Jellyfish

Bobbing in the water
like
a
dream-
er.
Your tentacles dangle
down
below
as
you
swim away the day.

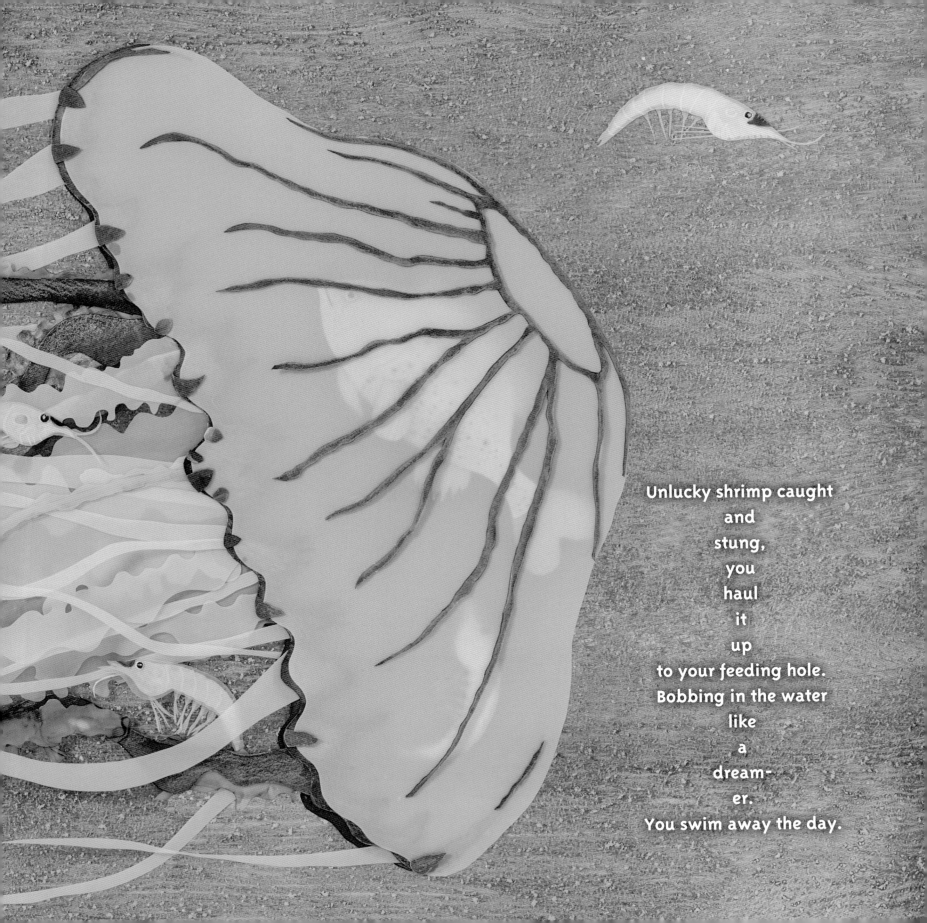

Unlucky shrimp caught
and
stung,
you
haul
it
up
to your feeding hole.
Bobbing in the water
like
a
dream-
er.
You swim away the day.

Narwhal

Begin
a twenty-five-minute dive
down
below the light—
one thousand feet.

Your whale sounds
probe the deep—
down
two thousand feet.

Your blubber lining
keeps you safe from cold—
down
three thousand feet.

Squeaking and whistling
and armed with a tusk-tooth,
you suck up dinner
down
on the ocean floor.

Time is running.
It's a long way back
up
to where you began—
up
to air—
up
where you must go
to breathe and live.

Piranha

Piranha is a toothy fish—
its jaws, they open wide.

Best to be some other place
and not become its meat.

Piranha is a toothy fish—
its jaws, they open wide.

When piranha's on the hunt,
you're wise if you retreat.

Piranha is a toothy fish—
its jaws, they open wide.

Otter

Long whiskers,
sensitive paws,
probing after
shellfish, mussel, clam.

Finding a
just-right rock,
to break open
stubborn shells
that conceal
their treats.

Takes a lot
to feed an otter—
fine dining
on the water.

Aardvark

Beware
the aardvark's claws that dig,
that sticky tongue,
the snout that pries.

Beware
when aardvark's hungry.
It does no good
to crawl down holes.

No matter
how you try to hide—
you can't.

Koala

Mostly what I do is chew—
    and chew
        and chew and . . .
            sleep.

And wake and chew—
    and chew
        and chew and . . .
            sleep.

Eucalyptus leaves are yummy,
but they need time
inside my tummy.

So mostly what I do is chew—
    and chew
        and chew and . . .
            sleep.

African Bush Elephant

Along the glade's forest edge,
at work in summer's skimpy shade—
your trunk stretches high,
tears leaves from limbs.

Eager mouth opens,
brick-size teeth smash and shred.
Belly rumbles, welcomes
another wad of leaves
dropping in.

Hippopotamus

He eats at night
along the bank—
filling his giant needs
with lips that pull up
reeds and grass.
Enormous mouth
stretches wide,
shows teeth like spikes.

No one ever called
a hippo sweet.
Truth is
   he's ill-tempered.
And consider this:
unless you run faster
than nineteen miles per hour,
don't provoke him.
He'll cross a river
side to side
before you have a chance
to say "I'm sorry."

FLYING EATERS

Turkey Vulture

Thinks that meat's a treat, all rotten.
Loves roadkill, sun-grilled au gratin.

Tears out chunks to fill its belly
at every roadside smelly deli.

Dines on putrid filth and worms.
Doesn't mind the nasty germs.

Gut's so strong it can't get sick
on rancid bites gone slimy-slick.

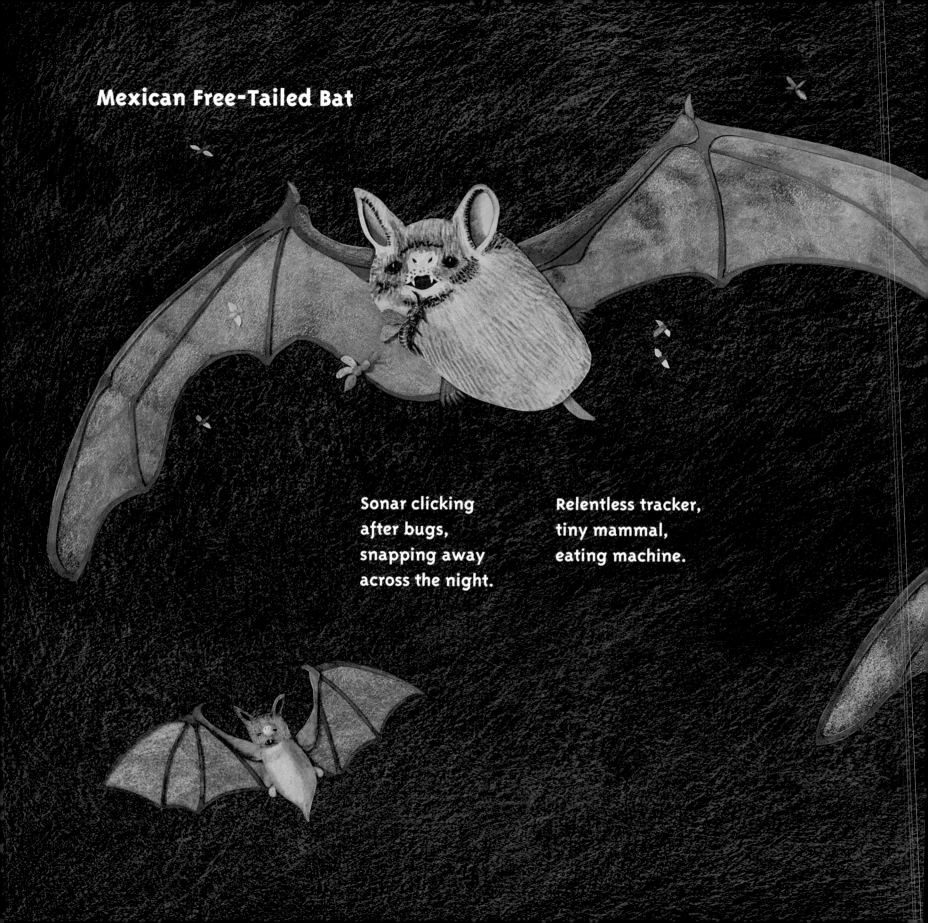

Mexican Free-Tailed Bat

Sonar clicking
after bugs,
snapping away
across the night.

Relentless tracker,
tiny mammal,
eating machine.

Night's work done,
sonar-guided
back through
hidden crack
in cavern wall.

Belly full,
food digesting,
upside down,
time to rest.

Housefly

Fly walk
 across your meal.
 Taste it with your
fly-tongue toes.
 Soften it with your
fly-vomit spit.
 Suck it through your
fly-tube mouth.
 Dodge the swatter!
 Escape to
fly walk
 across your next meal.
 Disgusting if you aren't a fly;
fly-like
 if you are.

Seagull

Few with feathers
find more ways
to fill their bill.

Darting fish,
leaping shrimp,
bug snatched in flight,
mouse,
bird,
bites of whale—
dead or alive—
and food from stashes
shaded by beach umbrellas.

Armed with the power
to drink salt water,
a gull dives for fish,
octopus, shrimp.

Creature of air, land, sea,
few with feathers
find more ways
to fill their bill.

SWIMMING EATERS

Jellyfish *Medusozoa*

There are many kinds of jellyfish and sea jellies. Some can move by contracting their body to push through the water. Others float wherever the currents take them. There are tiny ones no bigger than a human thumbnail, and there are giants that weigh hundreds of pounds. Below an umbrella-shaped, often colorful body, many kinds of jellyfish dangle delicate stinging tentacles, some more than one hundred feet long. Jellyfish venom can be deadly. Small fish, shrimp, or other jellyfish that blunder into tentacles are paralyzed and then slowly hauled up and eaten.

Narwhal *Monodon monoceros*

The small whale called the narwhal is known for its single tusk, which is really a long tooth. It is called "the unicorn of the sea." But what makes this creature unique is where it eats. It's a mammal, so it has to breathe air. But it feeds on the Arctic seafloor, sometimes close to a mile below the surface. How is this possible? The narwhal has developed a flexible neck, echolocation (sounds) to help it find food in the deep dark ocean, and thick blubber to protect it from the water's frigid temperatures. Not only that, it can hold its breath for up to twenty-five minutes, enough time to reach the bottom of the ocean, suck up the types of fish and squid that live deep, and return to the surface for air.

Piranha *Serrasalmidae*

Piranhas are usually less than one foot long and are armed with some of the sharpest teeth in the world. In spite of their fearsome reputation, these South American fish feed mostly on insects, other fish, crustaceans, worms, carrion (dead animals), and even seeds and plants. Piranhas swim in packs and can attack in force, but scientists believe they stay together mostly to protect themselves from larger animals. Piranhas make sounds, such as short barks and low grunts, to warn creatures to get out of their way. Good advice!

Otter *Enhydra lutris*

The sea otter has the densest fur of any animal, which protects it from cold water when it dives down for food on the ocean floor. The otter can catch fish with its quick forepaws, but it prefers

shellfish. Sensitive whiskers and strong claws help it find and dig up its prey. An otter has the ability to use rocks as tools, something few other animals can do. It finds a stone and knocks abalone shells off of submerged rocks, and it uses small rocks to break open shellfish, such as mussels. An otter also has pockets of loose skin under each foreleg to carry its catch, and its teeth are designed for crushing.

LEARN MORE!

Clarke, Ginjer L. *Jellyfish*! New York: Penguin Young Readers, 2021.

Osborne, Mary Pope. *Narwhals and Other Whales.* New York: Random House, 2020.

Levy, Janey. *Piranhas Bite!* New York: Gareth Stevens Publishing, 2020.

Marsh, Laura. *Sea Otters.* Washington, DC: National Geographic Kids, 2014.

Use the library or internet to find out more.

LAND-BASED EATERS

Aardvark *Orycteropus afer*

The aardvark, which lives in sub-Saharan Africa, feeds mostly on ants and termites and can eat fifty thousand of them in one night. It uses a long snout filled with special nerves to smell prey underground and strong curved claws to dig out dinner. Its nostrils close up to keep dust and insects out of its snout. The aardvark traps insects with its foot-long tongue covered in sticky saliva and swallows them whole. Strong stomach muscles grind the food. A thick hide protects this hunter from bites and pinches. Long ears help detect predators such as lions, hyenas, and pythons while the aardvark feeds.

Koala *Phascolarctos cinereus*

Eucalyptus leaves are tough, have little nutritional value, and are poisonous to most animals. But the cuddly looking Australian koala has developed special ways to thrive on them. Its teeth are designed to nip off leaves and cut them into bite-size pieces. The koala has a much bigger cecum (SEE-kum) (part of the intestine) than other animals, which allows its body to better break down the leaves and poison into food it can use. Because digestion takes so long, the koala gets good nutrition from the leaves. And by sleeping up to twenty hours each day, koalas conserve energy while digesting.

African Bush Elephant *Loxodonta africana*
When you're about ten feet tall and weigh twelve thousand pounds, you need a lot of food and water. The largest land animal has unique ways to get its fill. The African bush elephant's upper lip and nose combine to form a strong flexible trunk, which acts like a hand, hose, and lifter. Its tusks are actually modified incisor teeth that can strip away bark and gouge into the ground for water and minerals. The elephant's brick-size teeth break down wood and leaves, and its large stomach can digest the enormous meals it eats to stay healthy.

Hippopotamus *Hippopotamus amphibius*
Hippos of sub-Saharan Africa love water and spend much of their day there, often napping with only their face showing. Males are bigger than females, and average weights are between three and six thousand pounds. Hippos need a lot of food, but they don't care for water plants. So they come ashore at night to graze on reeds, grass, and green shoots. Over time they have developed long front teeth for cutting and enormous, flat back teeth for grinding. Hippos have three sections in their stomach, which helps them digest food. They differ from cows, sheep, and other ruminants (animals with multi-section stomachs) because hippos don't chew cud, but instead let their stomach do the digesting.

LEARN MORE!

Nelson, Penelope S. *Aardvarks*. Minneapolis, MN: Jump! / Bullfrog Books, 2019.

Szymanski, Jennifer. *Climb, Koala!* Washington, DC: National Geographic Kids, 2017.

Bishop, Nic. *Elephants*. New York: Scholastic, 2022.

Murray, Julie. *Hippopotamus*. Minneapolis, MN: Dash! / Abdo Zoom, 2021.

Use the library or internet to find out more.

FLYING EATERS

Turkey Vulture *Cathartes aura*

A turkey vulture circling in the sky uses its keen eyesight and excellent sense of smell to search for its meals. It prefers animals that haven't been dead for long, but foul-smelling, putrid carcasses will also do. The vulture is a cesspool of poison, viruses, bacteria, fungus, and mold. Its head, beak, and stomach are coated with deadly germs, but the vulture has a digestive system that breaks down many kinds of poisons inside its gut.

Mexican Free-Tailed Bat *Tadarida brasiliensis*

There are more than one thousand kinds of bats. Some eat fruit, some like nectar, and a few suck blood. But most bats, such as the Mexican free-tailed bat, eat insects. To locate their food while they fly, they use a special sonar called echolocation. As bats come out at dusk and hunt through the night, they make high-pitched sounds that humans can't hear. The sounds bounce off prey, and the bat closes in and swallows in flight. The same echolocation helps the bat find its way back home to a safe place to rest during the daytime.

Housefly *Musca domestica*

There are more than 160,000 known kinds of flies in the world, and most of us are familiar with the housefly. Two small antennae on its head are covered with tiny hairs that can smell food from long distances. The fly uses hairs on its feet to taste, similar to the way humans use taste buds in our mouth. A housefly vomits chemicals from its stomach onto food to soften it up, then sucks it through its mouth. Houseflies can be carriers and spreaders of disease.

Seagull *Laridae*

Seagulls are the most widespread seabird in the world. They are at home walking, swimming, and flying. A gland near their nostrils lets them drink and digest salt water (only a small group of birds can). Being able to drink salt water helps them dive in the ocean for fish, clams, and mussels. Seagulls are smart creatures known for dropping heavy shells onto rocks to break them open. Gulls are noisy, fearless, and don't hesitate to steal human treats. They eat a wide range of food, which helps them survive in a variety of habitats.

LEARN MORE!

Dunn, Mary R. *Turkey Vultures*. Mankato, MN: Capstone Press, 2015.

Riggs, Kate. *Bats*. Mankato, MN: Creative Education, 2020.

Heavenrich, Sue. *13 Ways to Eat a Fly*. Watertown, MA: Charlesbridge, 2021.

Pulley Sayre, April. *Seagulls Soar*. New York: Astra Young Readers, 2020.

Use the library or internet to find out more.

NOT AN EATER AT ALL

Mayfly

The mayfly doesn't
bite or
chew or
pinch or
tear or
drink.
It can't.

It lives only
a single day.
No need
for a mouth.
It needs only
to find a mate.

Mayfly *Ephemeroptera*

Adult mayflies have adapted to eat nothing at all. Some kinds live for one day in maturity. Others live only a few minutes. The insects come swarming up from lakes and rivers, sometimes by the millions, looking to mate in midair before they die. But young mayflies, called nymphs, live underwater for up to two years, and they do eat. Mostly they nibble water plants and forms of algae, nourishing their bodies until it's time to change form, swim to the surface, fly, and find a mate.